CW00539418

SAMARKAND, AND OTHER MARKETS I HAVE KNOWN

Wole Soyinka was born in Nigeria in 1934. He was educated at Government College, Ibadan and then at England's Leeds University, and worked in British theatre before returning to Nigeria in 1960. His earlier prose works include *The Interpreters*, which was awarded the Jock Campbell Prize for Commonwealth Literature. Wole Soyinka received a New Statesman John Whiting Award for 1966–7 and was Overseas Fellow at Churchill College, Cambridge, in 1973–4, where he wrote the widely acclaimed *Death and the King's Horseman*. He has been awarded the George Benson Medal of the Royal Society for Literature and the UNESCO Medal for the Arts. In 1986 he became the first African writer to win the Nobel Prize for Literature. Forced into exile in 1994 by military dictatorship, he returned home four years later and now divides his time between Nigeria and overseas universities.

WOLE SOYINKA

—

SAMARKAND

and Other Markets I Have Known

Methuen

Methuen

1 3 5 7 9 10 8 6 4 2

This collection published in Great Britain in 2002 by
Methuen Publishing Limited
215 Vauxhall Bridge Road
London SW1V 1EJ

Methuen Publishing Limited Reg. No. 3543167

A CIP catalogue record for this book is available from the British Library

ISBN 0 413 77255 1

Typeset by Deltatype Ltd, Birkenhead, Merseyside

Printed and bound in Great Britain by
Creative Print and Design (Wales) Ltd, Ebbw Vale

CONTENTS

Outsiders

AH, DEMOSTHENES!   3
PENS FOR HIRE   5
HOURS LOST, HOURS STOLEN   7
BUSINESS LUNCH – THE BAG LADY   10
DOCTORED VISION   14

Of Exits

SOME DEATHS ARE WORLDS APART   19
EXIT LEFT, MONSTER, VICTIM IN PURSUIT
    (DEATH OF A TYRANT)   21
WHERE THE NEWS CAME TO ME OF THE DEATH
    OF A TYRANT   23
EXIT   25
CALLING JOSEF BRODSKY FOR KEN SARO-WIWA   26

Fugitive Phases

LOST POEMS   33
IN THE SMALL HOURS   35
VISITING TREES (NIGHT HUNT)   36

The Sign of the Zealot

TWELVE CANTICLES FOR THE ZEALOT . . .   43
SAMARKAND, AND OTHER MARKETS I HAVE KNOWN   49

Elegies

THE CHILDREN OF THIS LAND   63
TOWER CLOCK: AKE REVISITED   65
LOW-COST HOUSING   67
ELEGY FOR A NATION   68
VAIN RANSOM   78

Outsiders

AH, DEMOSTHENES!

I shall ram pebbles in my mouth
Demosthenes
Not to choke, but half dolphin, half
Shark hammerhead from fathoms deep
Ride the waves to charge the breakers
They erect,
Crush impediments of power and inundate
Their tainted towers –
I shall ram pebbles in my mouth.

I shall place nettles on my tongue
Demosthenes
Then thwart its stung retraction. Oh,
Let it burn at root and roof
Let rashes break from every pore
Just so it sear the tyrant's power
With one discharge
I shall place nettles on my tongue.

But have you heard of *werepe*
Demosthenes?
Not all your Stoics' calm can douse
The fiery hairs of that infernal pod.
It makes a queen run naked to the world
An itch that tells the world its flesh
Is whorish sick –
I shall place *werepe* on every tongue.

I'll drop some ratsbane on my tongue
Demosthenes
To bait the rodents with a kiss of death

3

I'll seal their fate in tunnels dark and dank
As habitations of their hostages
Denied of air, denied of that same light
Their hands had cupped to immerse their world
I'll drop some ratsbane on my tongue.

I'll thrust all fingers down the throat
Demosthenes
To raise a spout of bile to drown the world.
It's petrified, Demosthenes, mere forms,
Usurp the hearts we knew, mere rasps.
This stuttering does not become the world,
This tongue of millions fugitive from truth –
I'll thrust all fingers down the throat.

I'll let the hemlock pass
Demosthenes –
Oh, not between my lips – I've shared
Its thin dissolve in myriad throats
At one with that agnostic sage.
They did not stutter like the world they left –
And I know why –
Their lives were spent with heated pebbles
On their tongues, Demosthenes!

PENS FOR HIRE

The pen may beat a path to ploughshares
Pen beat ploughshares into swords
In words from ploughshare and the sword.
And pen enshrine, and pen unmask the lies
Of vain mythologies, pen enthrone
The mouldy claims of Power, urge
Contested spaces as divinely given.

Pen prove mighty ear of swords
Glory tongue of gory deeds, dress rape
In fame, plunder in time-honoured robes
Of epic deeds. The pen may dip
In ink-well and, emerging,
Drip with blood.

Precious stones adorn their tongues of rote,
Of cant, of sterile incantation.
Show me the water beds they lie upon
Pull the plug and puzzle why the flow is darkened red
And thick, and clotted. Eternally

In swarm as locusts, as lies and flies, consorts
Drawn to dark orgies of commemorating pens –
Long is the line of great seductions
Lure of ease within our chequered tribe – from griots
Of voice, to plume, and the compact processor.
Some, we have come to know. They served
And were served in turn. Some believed,
And others cashed their souls in make-believe.

But both are immunised against the testament
Of eyes, and ears, the stench and guilt of power
And anomy of reddening rain, of plagues of locusts,
Deaths of firstborns, seven lean years and
Yet again the eighth and sequent round –
Of death and dearth. A pledge not earned or given
Is not in mortals to redeem –

But God decreed the end shall multiply the means –
A seasoned waiter, the pen inscribes:
We also serve.

HOURS LOST, HOURS STOLEN

Why lament: is it lost time? Days irretrievable?
Why play the cards of time with vain resentment
And thus augment the deficit imposed
By usurper hands in stolen spaces?

Hands that spurn acknowledgement of debt to earth
That spawned and nurtured them,
Shun bonds of kin, mock pride of race
Devoid of thought that seeks renewal
For each day's depletion, for community's
Creeping senescence, premature decay.

Theirs are the minds that breed the virus of loss
Theirs the agency of our untimely death.

Witching hour, opaque passage into dawn.
Appointments surge you do not wish to keep
The heartbeat riots, the brain in panic,
Strives to marshal order from the rival ranks of
'Must do', 'Can't do', 'Hate to', 'Won't do',
But soon confronts the malignant prowler
That slinks around the peripheries of sleep
Awaiting consciousness to recommence
Its feast on time – in duty's masquerade.

An earthquake would be welcome arbiter,
A cosmic convulsion, a gloating *deus ex machina*
To impose their own disorders on disordered minds
And land. Sooner this, than that which lurks beyond the
    door
That must be unfastened, waits to drain the mind anew

And test the will. But Nature is indifferent, defers
To human hands for a grim efficiency of waste.

These jackals only seem at bay, or in retreat.
A new pack is regrouping just beyond the brush
The cackle is familiar, no remorse. They know
The trees against whose bark their hind legs
Were last raised – they home in on their odours.
Daylight will flush them out, not chase them home
The future may reject, and memories deny them –
But now, they kill us slowly, from shrine to township.
They kill us slowly on farmstead, in ivory towers
And factories. They kill our children in their cribs.

The landscape alters, the landscabs remain. Trees give way
To lamp-posts on the urine trail. Their mangy whelps
Will follow soon, and learn the sterile strut.
A pall of stench descends upon the land, a stillness
Of the fear of millions crouched behind their doors.

They kill us slowly here, slowly, and sometimes
Multiply, several times over, kill us
Brutally, with mindless glee, kill us
With void, with phrases that mimic motion
Kill with time abuse, with mind abuse. Kindness
Is out of fashion. Reputation is sold as staple
Of coated tongues, corrosive teeth,
Ingested at dawn, regurgitated at noon.

Willing ears fulfil the rancid mind
And fantasies pollute the air, piling
Ordure on ordure. Reality intrudes,
And finds the palate jaded. Power moves
To fill vacated spaces. The captive race
Succumbs to oiled mechanics of the superior lie.

Why ponder the lost hours, and years?
We know which way they flew, what leeches –
Native only for the soil that suckled them –
Sank sly probosces deep in open veins
And piped our life blood through indifferent seas.
To vaults impregnable, beyond recall, safe
From devaluation. Leftovers serve the rest.
From tanks of septic broth their hands have stirred,
They bid the nation slurp.

They kill us slowly with force-feeding – a diet of force.
They kill us slowly temporising – thieves of time.
The landscape wilts from discharges of their hind legs
Our space is sucked into the void of their existence.

Go now, *school in the wiles of the thief, appropriate*
The apothecary of poisoners. Learn fawning,
Master the backward bow and crawl, but – preach charity
That feeds the hand it'll bite – serve obsequiousness
As their last supper and their obsequies.

BUSINESS LUNCH – THE BAG LADY

for Femi Johnson

It was an afternoon of indifferent news
The world was still, the world was turbid
The Dow Jones index fell several points
Or rose – to a Wall Street dunce, all
Trading leads to bankruptcy or wealth
And there an end.

The babble of striped suits, lunching
On expense accounts left him cold.
He only wished his host had chosen differently,
Feeling lost among the tinkle of glass cubes
In iced teas, gurgle of – predictable – Chardonnay –
I have to return to work, well, just another –
And the sudden welt of laughter that
Somehow traced the downward spiral
Of some absent victim, a hollow victory,
Or simply a dirty joke. Suddenly –

One false note among the staid discordance,
A rogue painting, lone in the gallery of fakes.
Ignored, a highlight through the stain of laughters
That sought refuge in rendition of the intruder as
Invisible, barely spied through opacities of
Bonhomie, joie de vivre . . . beneath the false
Banter – *now, what has this place become?*

I did not see her enter.
So still, her gaze implacably wound
In thought, yet, a laser beam through
The noon window. Not quite a tramp,

And yet, a misfit in her bulbous wrap.
A handbag held her secrets, safe
In line of vision on the table top, to a micro world
Of her mobile home without, a shopping cart
Piled high with a lifetime foraging.

Does she feel eyes, and shuffling feet
And swivelling heads, arrested Martinis
Midway to genteel throats? She does not fidget.
No Morse code filters through her feet
Cased in soft-leather ease, to read impatience.
An ankle of white socks beneath
Stovepipe jeans, faded – or distressed –
She waited. Angled feet, anxiety deprived,
Mildly wrapped around the table stem
Affirmed her equipoise.
Not comfort seeking, it was just
Her way of sitting, limbs that find
And nuzzle those of a now familiar lover.

Awesomely at ease, oblivious
To the inner room on which her back was turned,
Unperturbed by the kaleidoscope without –
Does she note the Labrador on leash, hind leg raised
In wet salute against a caged sapling?
Her pebble lenses yield no clue, her gaze
Is innocence itself, and when the waiter bends
A practised ear, a face conceding no surprise,
Her order is precise, assured –

As grew the demolition when the rack
Of lobsters came and *tabula rasa* turned
A rapturous field in one transcendent flash.

Then came the love affair. A tease, a foreplay
A realignment of limbs and mock passes
With steel nutcrackers over prostrate
Yet aggressive curvatures. When it came,

The crunch was massive – as the silence drawn
In turned heads and suspended gestures.
Eyes turned to floundering fish. Then, claw by claw,
She tamed the rash crustacean, probed
Deep crevices for virgin flesh, teased out
Sleek slivers, inaccessible till then.
The dainty prong between her fingers
Was a tuning fork.

                    And thus it was
That sounds of breaking surf
Overwhelmed a beach of loud sun-worshippers
A diviner's stick that plumbed the arid
Carapace for unsuspected spurts
Of moisture, liposuctions coming
Fast but moderated, a narrative of barnacles
And limpets, deep-sea odysseys and Neptune's
Trident playfully at work in lyric fingers.

Her face, a surgeon's mask, still soft,
An infinite capacity for care and skilled sufficiency
Now assumed the lobster's ruddy glow.
Gently as a beaching craft, she coasted home,
Her legs released the prisoner stem
Hands fell away from conquered plates
Heaped shards of shell, self-surmounting
In their cream and prickle-red submission.

It was plain – she too had come for business!

It was an afternoon of indifferent news
The world was still, the world was turbid.
I had great need of a universe that still
Was peopled, lived, loved and died, ate
And defecated, wrapped its legs around a table stem.
The Labrador on leash returned without
A glance at its pliant urinal. Two nursemaids
Paused by the window, laughed and gossiped as in
A silent film. I turned inwards to a room
Filled suddenly with mouths and throats in thrall
To food as sometime function, saw my face reflected
In the wall-length mirror. Chastened now,
I gulped my tepid glass of – *Chardonnay.*

DOCTORED VISION

Submissive to the years' constraints
The poet tries again the optician's expertise.
The placard test begins. One eye
Obeys all semiotic tests. The other
Blurs the dots, rapes simple 'rithmetic –
The mind can only total what it separates –
But spots the gnat slow-crawling on the lens' eye.

Next, the literacy test – 'We'll try this board,
Shall we? Start with the topmost line.'
The errant eye discerns, at best
A charming alphabestiary. 'K'
Flaunts wings, 'R' wags a furry tail,
'H' sprouts horns, 'F' is unicorn.
Rabbit ears adorn the simple 'U' while udders
Droop from 'W'. 'C' has long closed ranks –
He thinks of flawed 'O' rings – *Am I*
Doomed to crash from vaulting vision?

The left eye, boastful, reads in sync.
The micro-printing on the bottom line
But finds the page, close held,
A mindless hieroglyphic smear!

The doctor frowns, tugs at his lower lip.
His scrutiny suggests a catch –
'They are *both* your eyes?
I know of no eye transplant in entirety.'

His sigh is terminal, he tells the poet
What other clinics had long diagnosed –

Short-sighted in one eye, long in the other.
The patient waits, the explosion comes on cue –
'But not within the limits we call natural!
A little difference, that's the norm, but this?
These, sir, belong to different pairs of eyes!'

Shrunken shanks, hoary head,
Will I look cute in monocle?

The poet plants, he hopes, a veto on
The optician's line of thought –
'I hate bi-focals.' The doctor's laugh
Is bitter. 'Your case, sir, goes beyond
Bi-focal remedy. Christ! You think I spend
Three hours on every client? With eyes like yours
No one could stay in business. A squint
Would make some sense, because your eyes, sir,
Are at war with one another. They harmonise
At certain magic intervals – don't ask me how.
They are your eyes, not mine – or so you claim.'
A sharp, derisive snort affirms the doubt.

Magic intervals? The patient feels consoled,
No longer isolated as a visual freak.
'That sounds poetic,' he reflects – 'harmonise
At magic intervals. All other clinics
Diagnose a bane. None, till now,
Has found a virtue in my visual cross.
You make it sound akin to poetic vision.'

The doctor's voice is strained. 'My cross, sir,
Is to find the right prescription for your sight.
Myopia, astigmatism, etc. – those modes of vision
Fill my register. There is NO poetic vision!'

The buzzer from front desk recalls him
To his waiting patients. His shoulders sag.
'Come back tomorrow. I may summon
A second opinion. The receptionist will find
A vacant slot, I hope. One slot? Best make it
Three. Or five. Maybe we should allot
One entire morning to your case. Yes,
A second opinion. Two heads are better than one.'

His laugh, the patient thinks, sounds faintly
Manic – 'ha ha . . . two heads . . . yes, in your case
How true! Four eyes, the perfect answer . . .
Sixteen combinations – that should cover
All your magic intervals.'

Behind the doctor's antiseptic stare
The patient reads experimental lust
And flees the clinic, never to return.
Today he roams the streets, surviving
On his own prescription:

One eye-patch woven of gossamer skeins
From that charmed loom that spun
Images of new clothes for the Emperor.
And, for the other eye, a conjured prism, herding
Riots of signals into a parsimonious
Lyric impetus, spaced, at magic intervals.

Of Exits

SOME DEATHS ARE WORLDS APART

*for Kudirat**

No bed of flowers bloomed for Kudirat
She was not royal, white or glamorous
Not one carnation marked the spot of death.
Though undecreed, a ban on mourning spoke
Louder than cold-eyed guns that spat
Their message of contempt against the world.

Oh, there were noises from the diplomatic world
A protest diskette ran its regulation course – but
She was no media princess, no sibling
Of hagiomanic earls. All too soon it was:
Business as usual. Dark sludge
And lubricant of conscience, oil
Must flow, though hearts atrophy, and tears
Are staunched at source.

Death touches all, both kin and strangers.
The death of one, we know, is one death
One too many. Grief unites, but grief's
Manipulation thrusts our worlds apart
In more than measurable distances – there are
Tears of cultured pearls, while others drop
As silent stones. Their core of embers
Melts brass casings on the street of death.

* Kudirat Abiola was the wife of the elected Nigerian President M.K.O.
Abiola, who was assassinated by agents of the usurping dictator,
Sanni Abacha, in June 1996, the year before Princess Diana died in a
motor accident.

She was not royal, white or glamorous
No catch of playboy millionaires.
Her grace was not for media drool, her beauty
We shall leave to nature's troubadours.

Courage is its own crown, sometimes
Of thorns, always luminous as martyrdom.
Her pedigree was one with Moremi,
Queen Amina, Aung Sung Kyi, with
The Maid of Orleans and all who mother
Pain as offspring, offer blood as others, milk.

She seeks no coronet of hearts, who reigns
Queen of a people's will.
Oh let us praise the lineage
That turns the hearth to ramparts and,
Self surrendered, dons a mantle that becomes
The rare-born Master of Fate.

EXIT LEFT, MONSTER, VICTIM IN PURSUIT

Death of a Tyrant

Long, long before he slipped
Viagra
Down his throat, and washed it down
With 3-Barrel rotgut,
His favourite gargle from Iganmu,*
Libelled home-made brandy as in
Home-made democracy, the Gunner
Was a goner.

The world said he'd outgunned
The finest and the best
Of a hundred million but
The Gunner was long gone.

For once, the game of substitutes
Was perfect, truly
Impeccable – as in *non*
Peccavi – without reproach.
His last thought was: a strange taste
To this familiar pill, concluding:
A stronger dosage, as befits a despot –
Pleased he was.

The Gunner's gone
Who leap-frogged boundaries to restore
What he withheld at source.
But killing is but half the game
And must ignite the question: in whose cause
Was this neat killing made?

* A Nigerian distillery

To end a nation's agony? Or as nettled will –
Putting the once faithful dog to sleep
That has turned rabid?

The answer came on cue.
A month of victory chants turned
Curses on a million tongues.
It was a blasphemous equation –
The killers took the one on whom
A nation's hopes were vested.
The field, they gloated, was now levelled.

The Gunner's gone
Who never faced his foes
But took them from the rear
His targets – women (Kudirat *et al*)
Octogenarians – Alfred Rewane – and
Once-faithful servitors now mired
In the Gunner's fears
Entrapped as flies in spotty webs
The Gunner spun at whim.

Though wigged and gowned in places, Justice
Is no coated pill, administered
In clinical conspiracies. The game
Of substitution works only when
Justly made. A capsule may consume more than
The heart that's stopped.

The Borgias come to mind
In this twentieth-century tale –
Of poisoned rings and coated chalices
A Grand Guignol that yet awaits
The happy ending of a fairy tale.

WHERE THE NEWS CAME TO ME OF THE
DEATH OF A TYRANT

Dusk on Mount of Olives, Noble Sanctuary,
I stood, medium of a nation's darkest hour,
Stranger, as so many feet, to a sere land
Peopled also by strangers – journeys shared
On legendary paths, epic wells, patriarch cemeteries,
Rites, reliquaries, and holy sanctuaries – bound
At navel, yet strangers sworn to sword. Mine also
Was the darkest hour of a distant land.

No wonder, the sinuous plains, far as eyes or mind
Could capture, ruptured suddenly, filled with sparks
Of scythe-hubbed chariots, impassioned lances,
Froth-lipped horses in the charge of death,
Riders, salvation bound in one last holy carnage.
The ghosts of old delusions, potent still, revelled
In invocation of the Sacred Word. Had time
Stood still for this birthland of millennia?

A blindfold, wider than nations and more craved
Stretched, it seemed, across spires and domes,
Cross and crescent, toned in the golden haze of dusk,
Snaked through bronze warrens, spice and leather alleys,
Date trestles, sandalwood, olive groves and sparse oases,
Wound through catacombs where piety preys and wounds.

Yet the air was peace, palpable to touch,
An eternal presence like a set transparency
Masking the face of gore, a resolution glimpsed
Through palimpsests of blood-stained suns.

A gift it proved, a resolution dearly sought. Strife
Brought me to a warring land, where olives
Detonate in shrapnels, shrivel as infant heads,
Hope is split on the axe of history, zeal, and politics.
Yet one road only leads to Jerusalem, only one –
That broad, pebbled spine of human oneness.

Pondering war, I trod the sandal-paved stones
Senses lulled in light incense, brushed by hems
Of robes from distant sages, pilgrims of all faiths.
And the dark hour beckoned to me in hope.
From that seared land that I had sworn
I would not leave with empty hands, came a gift
And a choice to amplify, or squander. One tyrant less
May spell little, but who scorns the miser's dole
Of respite, a drop of manna from skies of that same
Miracle land. One drum of war, at least, was muted.

This gift lies heavy on my hands, unrequited.
Would I could stay the glimpse of that rare moment
When the shrouds of history parted, and a vision
Of hope suffused the plains of the Mount of Olives,
Noble Sanctuary.

EXIT

for François Mitterrand

All that could be done was done
The best of skills exhausted, no limits placed
On what the purse could buy. The rest
Was vanity. He called the learned to his side
To debate mortality. To his advocate dictated
'I bequeath . . .' For a world weaned on the *bon mot*,
Turned jester – 'I do not mind the face of death, but find
Not being around distasteful.'

But his physician was
Sole beneficiary of his Last Will and Testament.
'Like you, I seek release – you, of your Oath, I
Of mortality. Were I
To stop these time-delaying pills, would you
Find yours, and free from blame?' The answer being –
Yes – he quit.

CALLING JOSEF BRODSKY FOR KEN SARO-WIWA

This Joseph trod some strange paths, it would seem –
Stranger even than his namesake's, the dreamer's.
The same feet once condemned to plough
Through horse manure had also voyaged
To the frozen wastes, hands that shovelled shit,
Carved and stitched cadavers, had grasped the peak
Of glaciers. It read strange, but there it was,
Narrated in the Supplements' Obituaries.

I did not know him. We sometimes shared a podium,
The usual talking spaces stolen from real life.
I found him ill at ease, caught in vague bewilderment,
Inclined to drift beyond mere confines of a word,
A phrase, or pause. He wore his exile
Sparsely on his frame, a store-bought suit
Not custom fitted nor ill-fitting,
Simply alien, a cast-off piece from an Oxfam store –
Is this the outfitter we all must share before we die?

They claimed you were a symbol, in or out
Of *pro patria*. Your rulers disagreed. First:
Your velvet pants read – social parasite.
Guilty as charged? Another charge might read:
He trod manure, yet declared
His turd was his to shape at will, ejected
Pellets outside regulation forms – a claim
No equine orifice would dare conceive
Even in the land of all-wise Houyhnhnms.
Horses shit in social realism, dialectical
To the last neighing Nay, the whinnying
Aye-aye Comrade sir.

Moscow is cold. Ogoni is heated space
Where fires burn all day and night, and gases
Blacken fish and leaves from endless flues.
Still, death is death, and home is sometime exile
When lines are drawn by Party or by gun.
Regarding Kenule and his companions eight
For social realism, inscribe – realpolitik, and profit.
For parasite, read Pest – the functions are the same.
And were you not both guilty as pronounced?

Yahoo you, I hear you smile, you deem it just
To infect the nation's bowels,
A normal occupation for a parasite.
The charges, questions multiply but you withdraw –
Your mind has moved to mould a likeness of
The prosecutor's head in horse manure.
The judge records your furtive smile – another year;
A private gift from him above the Party line.

The Party of the Niger Delta rules by the barrel –
Oil and gun – a marriage made in heaven.
Market forces write the law, rigs and derricks
Scorch the landscape, livelihood and lives. Marionettes
In itchy uniforms salute and settle civil strife
On 'orders from above' – the only tongue they learn –
For oil must flow through land and sea
Though both be silted from contempt and greed.

It is a path of choice for all named dissidents
From Chechnya to Ogoniland
And we must learn the comedy of law
And even bear its fatal flaws. Some discern
The pulse within the glacier, others a lustrous

Heartbeat in the depths of mangrove sludge.
But all believe there lives that hidden seed
Within the rancid compost of their world, a diamond
Pressed to flame from dross of timelessness.
Impervious to all else, your gaze will
Fasten on that kindred grain, a live soul
Playing truant in a mound of waste.

Kenule also had his day in court, they claim,
Before they sent him dangling in the void.
His judges also fumed to note the smile.
They floundered in the mists of secret love
Between the man thought captive, and the seed
Burgeoning in rivulets of slick, breaking ground
In carbon pall, defying the laws
Of photosynthesis. You learn to do without the sun
Where dungeons are the only breeding grounds.

You will recall your namesake, the other archetype
(No, not symbol, there I find common ground with your
Failed Houyhnhnms) – I think often of that other
    archetype
He of the multi-coloured robe, dreamer and
Interpreter of dreams. The erstwhile tyrant
Ate the humble pie, recalled the dreamer's talent to state
    use.
He quit the dungeon, mapped a people's cause – but,
Let all beware the prophet. Beware the prophet
In and out of court. And prophet, oh, beware, beware!
For tyrants are as variegated as the prophet's quilt
And some may learn, while others cage in dread
Of learning. And killing is a leveller of both dunce
And sage – a gesture ends what is least understood.

I never really knew you. I cling to yours because
I own a closer death, a death that dared elude
Prophetic sight. Dreams we all share, but close
Presentiment, may hover round the head, invisible
To all it most concerns. We had become immune to
    dread.
Assailed by tortuous ways of evil we eschewed
The literal. The loop was patient, a suspended sentence
Hung over him, named Moses of Ogoniland.

I think of yours because I own that closer death
Too close to dirge, too bitter to lament.
He also spoke for multitudes. He touched, he led them
Out of torpor, staff in hand, a massive head,
A boulder destined to be split
To let spring water through polluted lands.
I owe that death a reckoning too close
To assuage with a brief lament. I play
The simple messenger, dared thus far
To link two kindred souls from worlds apart
In passage to the other world.

Death that takes brutally breeds restless souls.
You'll find him in a throng of nine, seeking landmarks.
His soul's violation, the weight of a task unfinished
May rob him of bearing yonder. Take his hand,
Lead him, and be led by him.

Fugitive Phases

LOST POEMS

I think sometimes of poems I have lost –
Maybe their loss it was that saved the world – still
They do get lost, and I recall them only
When a fragment levitates behind
Discarded invoices, the black-rimmed notice
Of a last goodbye, a birth, a wedding invitation
And other milestones of a lesser kind.

The moment torments – why? Beyond
An instant's passion, dubious flash –
Satori in a bar, taxi or restaurant, an airport
Waiting lounge – that births the scribble
On a stained napkin, what cast of the ephemeral
Once resonates, then spurns the mind
The morning after? All that survives

Mimics a wrinkled petal pressed
Between pages of long-discarded books.
A falling leaf trapped briefly by the passing sun
It flashes, a mere shard of memory
But filled with wistful accusations
Of abandonment. Too late,

No life to it. The book is closed
The moment's exultation or despair
Drowned in wine rivers, shrivelled
In suns of greater wars. I turn
These scrapbooks of a moment's truth
To cinders, their curlings curse in smoke –
Once more fugitive beyond recall
Of usurper's summons by
The morning after.

I think of voices I have lost, and touches,
The fleeting brush of eyes that burrows
Deep within the heart of need, the pledge
Unspoken, the more than acts of faith
That forge an instant world in silent pact
With strangers – deeper, deeper bonds
Than the dearest love's embrace.

IN THE SMALL HOURS

Blue diaphane, tobacco smoke
Serpentine on wet film and wood glaze,
Mutes chrome, wreathes velvet drapes,
Dims the cave of mirrors. Ghost fingers
Comb seaweed hair, stroke aquamarine veins
Of marooned mariners, captives
Of Circe's sultry notes. The barman
Dispenses igneous potions –
Somnabulist, the band plays on.

Cocktail mixer, silvery fish
Dances for limpet clients.
Applause is steeped in lassitude,
Tangled in webs of lovers' whispers
And artful eyelash of the androgynous.
The hovering notes caress the night
Mellowed deep indigo – still they play.

Departures linger. Absences do not
Deplete the tavern. They hang over the haze
As exhalations from receded shores. Soon,
Night repossesses the silence, but till dawn
The notes hold sway, smoky
Epiphanies, possessive of the hours.

This music's plaint forgives, redeems
The deafness of the world. Night turns
Homewards, sheathed in notes of solace, pleats
The broken silence of the heart.

VISITING TREES

Night Hunt

To step within a tree is not so arduous, indeed
No harder than thought, involuntary as
Walking, placing left foot after right, except
There are no limbs, not even a floating
Sensation – there is no body. You slip in
Eel-like, as into night's marsupial pouch –

But not in city parks, geometric avenues.
It helps perhaps that the child that was, once
Was prone to trespassing, climbing
To a vantage couch of barks and leaves
Broken shins on age-ring scabs, to marvel
At earth and sky, converse
With fleeting denizens of neither-nether world . . .

But only after a radar scan, alert frame
Swift to yield possession
To a hostile rustle, the slither of a snake, or simply
Dubious emanations at that time of day. But,

Sanctuary assured, monarch of time and space,
He is guardian to distant hives of human pulses.
Somewhere, he knows, life takes wing, floats past
On hair-thin filaments of detonating pods,
Enters or departs in ritual rounds of song and wind.
Antic celebrations of absences, he learns, are one
With the cyclic dance of renewal.

An assignation sometimes halts beneath his perch
Oblivious of the wide-eyed head, leaf-smothered

Now one with the accommodating heart of trees,
Their myriad moods of discord and embrace;
Or a farmer, homeward bound, whose way-station
This also is, bonded in a shared repose. A whiff
Of compost ascends from loam-caked pores
Stale with putrefaction, but steeped in growth.

His eyes turn lamps on the chamber of a chrysalis
Stuck to leaf or twig, dangling from dried mucilage.
He knows its history, this renewed pulsation,
Triumphant egress, clammy in birth fluids, flapping dry,
Then lifting on furry, variegated wings.

His pupillage was at the countless feet of that once
Millipede, witnessed its private solstice,
A strange paralysis whose myriad replications
Dangle from bark and leaf as miniature lanterns
Wicks unlit, awaiting dawn's arousal. All motion
Halted, till the drumroll of rains, a caesura
Between dark and light, called hibernation.
He guards the secret of the depleted sheath
Its translucent emptiness, visored as a seasonal
Masquerade, marked for disposition of the elements,

And is glad of sturdier walls and roof, a hearth
That beckons safety when the sky cracks, turns
Ink-wash, and birds urge flight. Still he delays
To open his throat to the skies, savour
Wind and rain on sensuous tongue, welcome
Their rounds of impassioned cleansing, rain fingers
Probing, seeding – and the future drawn deep
Into his breath, a tang of harvest and winnowing.

Those eyes grow deeper with the years, grow
Into seasons of glut and drought, frenzy and repose.
The youth that was, no longer climbs a tree
To seek admittance. The tree has swallowed him.
Superfluous is the limpet probe of ear against
Tree bark and boughs, yet the voice of sap
Flows friendly in his ears. Light and dark are emptied
Into vaulted passageways whose veins sprout
Side chambers as wine cellars hewn in cliffs. A glow
Without definition, neither oil lamp nor candlelight.
Nor even the dusk's filter. The only sound is the shush
Of sap in tune with earth's incessant rounds.

Some trees are thus, and ringed beyond mere count
Of ancestry or carbon dating. They heave
In nightly apotheosis, change their clothing
With the dawn, depleted. Their denizens have
Abandoned home, they throng the roads and markets,
Unremarked by human touch or eyes.

Their roots are ageless, washed by grand rivers.
Patriarchs, earth mothers, ministering priests
Of hills and plains, of mystic groves and healing presences.
All live in the immensity of timelessness. They open
To the night's dark fluorescence, not carnivorous
As some flowers, not sluts of night, garish in seduction.
They know their secrets were long yielded
To the guilelessness of youth. There is balm

In shadows of noon-framed trees, but these are
Literal, cast to distract the world. You must drink
Their night presence, on squirrel pads, breathing

The leaves' ferment, lit by glow-worms and the rank
Phosphorus of slinking fur. In the tree's dark throb,
A host awaits, offers rare ambrosia from its sacred vats.

The Sign of the Zealot

TWELVE CANTICLES FOR THE ZEALOT . . .

I

He wakes from a prolonged delirium, swears
He has seen the face of God.
God help all those whose fever never raged
Or has subsided.

II

Perched on church steeple, minaret, cupola
Smug as misericords, gleeful as gargoyles
On gables of piety, the vampire acolyte
Waits to leap from private hell
To all four compass points – but will not voyage alone.
His variant on the doctored coin reads: Come with me or –
Go to – *hell!*

III

He craves a parity
Beyond the contents of his skull.
A hundred thousand
Vacuities of mind are soon
Cowed beneath the grace and power
Of one gossamer quill – yet
Beware the mute! Beware the furtive power
Of the mutant's blade.

IV

The trade of healing takes strange turns.
Doctor and reservist, seeks the lethal path
To hearts of devotees in East Jerusalem,

Makes cadavers of believers turned
Eastwards in devotion – then turns the barrel
Inwards – still in hot pursuit?
For there are no post-mortems in the after-life
Though *rigor mortis* settles on the breath
Of peace.

V

They would be killers anyway, and anywhere.
Their world's a hiatus. Jerked to life,
They suck the teats of piety, briefly shed
A long cocoon of death. Dead eyes,
A death humility, death wish, dead end,
A death asymmetry that befits
A death-bound unbeginning.

Their mentors live, and thrive, instruct.
Behold their vengeance for a living death –
Wielding infantile gums but –
Teethed at school.

VI

It was his own kind, nailed
Yitzak Rabin to crossroads of the Orient
Arms extended to the Heights
Of peace. Across the Suez, the ghost
Of his precursor on the viewing stand
Watched the grim replay of a familiar reel.

VII

Ogun came riding through the streets
Of Jerusalem. The Chosen barred his way.

His bright metallic lore was profanation,
Railed the wandering tribe, custodian now
Of streets and pathways, closed on hallowed days
To songs of iron and steel, even a child's meandering
Bicycle, or infant's crib.

> Come war, will they deny
> The aid of iron? Come death
> Can they delay the caller's blade
> By plea of Sacred Feast?

The zealots' hands
Are stretched to rock the erring vehicle,
But not as rock the cradle of an infant peace.
Claws of hate, and clasp of closure reach
From pole to pole, embracing
Convertites of every faith. The maiming,
Killing act is all.

VIII

A god is nowhere born, yet everywhere.
But Rama's sect rejects that fine distinction –
The designated spot is sanctified, not for piety but –
For dissolution of yours from mine, politics of hate –
And forced exchange – peace for a moment's ecstasy.
They turn a mosque to rubble, stone by stone,
Condemned usurper of Lord Rama's vanished spot
Of dreamt epiphany. Now a cairn of stones
Usurps a dream of peace – can they dream peace
In iconoclast Uttar Pradesh?

IX

The meek shall inherit the earth . . .
Blessed are the peacemakers . . .
Shalom . . . Shalom . . . Shalom . . .
Irosu wonrin, irosu wonrin wonrin.
Salaam ailekum, ailekum
Shanti . . . shanti . . . shanti . . .
Oom . . . oom . . . oom . . . ooom . . .

Seek havens of peace on ocean floors,
Submarine depths, in lost worlds, black holes
Collapsed galaxies, in hermit caves
In jungle fastnesses and arctic wastes
Thorns of crowns and hairy shirts, beds of nails,
The saintly cheek that turns the other side, but –
Not in texts, not by learned rote. It's there
The unmeek prove inheritors of the earth.

They are the scripture grooms, possessive
To the last submissive dot. Punctilious
Guards of annotations, they sleepwalk blind to all
But the fatal hiatus:
Boom for *oom* and – sword for Word.
What is missing is – fulfilled!

X

Ile gbogbo nle orisa ee, ile gbogbo nle orisa
Ile gbogbo nle orisa ee, ile gbogbo nle orisa
Enia lo m'orisa w'aiye oo
*Ile gbogbo nle orisa ee**

Invent your god and forge his will
The home of piety is the soul.

I come from Ogun's land where
Women plant and teach and cure
Mould and build and cultivate,
Bestride the earth on sturdy thighs
Wipe sweat off open faces.
I come from Ogun's land where
Women spurn the veil, and men
And earth rejoice!

XI

Cast the sanctimonious stone
And leave frail beauty shredded in the square
Of public shame. This murder
Is the rock of sin, the wayward veil
A mere pebble's glint.

XII

Orunmila! Eleri ipin
Ibikeji Olodumare
Ajeju oogun
*Obiriti, Ap'ijo iku da . . .***
Some words are coarse, obscene, indecent.
They make a case for censorship, such words as
Pagan, heathen, infidel, unbeliever, kafiri, etc.
The cleric swears he'll sweep the streets clean
Of the unclean, armed with Book and Beard. Both
Turn kindling, but overturn the law of physics.
For the fire consumes all but the arsonist. He lives
To preach another day. The promised beast
Of the Apocalypse left me unbeliever
Till a rambling cleric apportioned death on CNN –
Surely that devil's instrument! – on Taslim Nazreem.
She wrote of an equalising God, androgynous
Who deals, ambidextrous, with the Left and Right.

XIII

. . . and a thirteenth for the merely superstitious.
This thirteenth canticle for you, and let
Ill-luck infest your dreams awhile, stress your fears.
Not one but both – Friday and thirteen
Joined to press the entry of my world
Onto *your* calendar. Would I could boast
A triple six, a Grand Slam by Satan's reckoning –
I would have long submerged the world
In cosmic laughter!

* All earth is the home of deities
  All earth is the home of deities
  It was mortals who brought the gods to the world
  All earth is home of deities

** Orunmila, Hand that apportions Fate
   Second only to the Supreme Deity
   He who swallows the potency of herbs
   Immense One, who turns aside the day of death

SAMARKAND, AND OTHER MARKETS
I HAVE KNOWN

for Naguib Mafouz

'The world is a market place . . .' – Yoruba song

'We take the Golden Road to Samarkand' –
James Elroy Flecker, *Hassan*

I

A market is kind haven for the wandering soul
Or the merely ruminant. Each stall
Is shrine and temple, magic cave of memorabilia.
Its passages are grottoes that transport us,
Bargain hunters all, from pole to antipodes, annulling
Time, evoking places and lost histories.

A market is where Samarkand invades
Johannesburg, and, as the shutters close,
Departs without regrets or trace
Until its next reincarnation. A market is
Where London's Portobello spells
Caracas and Yoruba, Catalan or Khourassan,
And though hard currency is what changes hands,
It lets you drift in fluid channels where
Sensations thrive on trade by barter.

Chimes of faith assail the market place –
The muezzin's prayer alert, a shrine within the warren,
A lean-to church dispenses chants at war
With handbells. White-robed dervishes in trance
At crossroads of Spices Row and Fabric Lane
Swirl, oblivious to slender saffron files

Meandering, equally oblivious to the world.
Fairy-bells in counterpoint to cosmic *ooms* –
Hare Krishna's other dervishes in slight
Ethereal motion through the firewood stalls.
Deep in the maze of Isale-eko,* Bhuddist mantras?

The *orisa* faithful wait their turn. In season,
Ogun's iron bells, Sango's *ayan* drums
Oya's chalk and coral maids reclaim
This borrowed space. Ancestral voice ascendant,
Masks of wood and webbed visors, indigo and camwood
Presences unfold their mats of invocation.

These are the markets I have known,
Tibetan souls on pilgrimage to shrines
In heartlands of Dogon, Baule or Zululand.
Leaflets of salvation for the unwary
Barefoot evangelists of every faith
Tuned to bared moments of the vacant soul.

Let all contend. Let a hundred thousand
Flowers diffuse exotic incense and a million
Stars perfume the sky, till the infant cry of Truth
Resound in the market of the heart,
And warring faiths
Reconcile in one immensity of Being.

Trade and holy places, saints and salesmen
Have ever lived as soul companions, caterers
For the needs of flesh and spirit – bread
And wafer, wine and holy water, homilies,
Talismans and rosaries, the blessed
Pouch of earth or magic mantras, locks
And lockets of painted mystics

* A Lagos suburb

Reliquaries and tourist souvenirs around
A healing spring, a spot of revelation –
The pilgrim trade is evenly sanctified.

Still, here and there, one lashes out – recall
The prince of peace turned manic in a synagogue
Turned market place? Lashed trespassers
With tongue and whip? That lash, in retrospect,
Was kind. I envy the usurers of old
The wages of their sin and mine. Our seasons'
Lesser desecrations – a face unveiled,
An ankle bared, a keepsake, taste or thought
Of *foreign* taint – feed Grim Reaper Purity
From lethal thrusts, not the symbolic lash.
They pierce the heart, not touch the soul within.

> *Go to the orisa and be wise. Ifa*
> *Shuns the excluding tongue, unveils*
> *Uncharted routes to knowledge, truth*
> *And godhead. Man is restless seeker,*
> *What follows six, says Ifa, transcends the bounds*
> *Of seven – there are no final rites to numerology.*
> *Let who can, count the motes in a sunbeam*
> *Or weigh the span of grief from voice to voice*
> *In the home of the immolated.*
> *Go to the orisa. None but fools*
> *Claim guardianship of the final gateway.*

II

Now – take a hidden turn between the stalls –
A curtain parts. The wares within are never on display
Ranged out of sight, awaiting clientele that know
The secret maps of every market place.

Fumes that ransack, then bare the mind
To ecstasies unknown in ancient Samarkand –
These seekers also ply uncharted routes
To the outer markets of the world, dissolve
In sunspots trapped in pin-points of their eyes,
Regaining wholeness only they know where.
Tubes and needles reign supreme. The crucible
Is sacrament and host to cravings
When the makeshift stove is lit.

Or enter where the sheen on beaten brass gives way
To a glint on the Gatling gun, still serviceable.
Or a shoulder-held dispatcher, lethal cone
On end, and oil wraps masking ingenuities
That pave the shortest way to hell. Still,
Hell's location is a space of choice. In open air,
Dante weds Fayed on ancient trestles
Browned with age, pages still uncut as if
To hide profanities of afterlife as dreamt
By poets and lunatics, moralists and lovers.
A slumbering virgin, timeless, but her youth preserved
And you the wandering prince to whom
Her thighs slit open for a gentle ravishing.

And Samarkand? O Samarkand!
I cannot stroll through markets but I dread
Lest I see Samarkand again, yet long to see
How exchange has merged with change, see
If the ageless geese on tattered slippers
In Utopia – the *lumpen prol.*, midwives
Of new breed of being, named the world's
Inheritors – have at last metamorphosed
Into princesses and masters of the promised land.

Such feeble scarecrows to my market mammas
Of Accra, Abidjan, Huambo, Cairo, Ibadan,
Plump mistresses of markets' riotous fare. Queens
Of fiesta, theatrics, courts of arbitration, crèche, but –
Wait! I summon witnesses to counter cries of bias:
Randy Weston, Oscar Peterson, hear them celebrate
Nigerian Marketplace, keyboards wild and wind on fire!
And strangers' brushes, daubing oils for dyes
In vain to trap the market's rainbow spectrum, bear
The weight of human tumult and the smell of life.
(It's there I pictured him, Mafouz, his soul in tune
With priests and pedlars of the *souk*.)

So much for ancient times – today the strings are muted.
Samarkand's sibling markets on these continents
Have fallen to dry dirges, dropped
To thin laments beneath collapsing thatch.
To make a killing on the market now
May prove too literal, where zealots strut as middlemen
To market lords of unseen paradise.

   III

O Samarkand. Remember Samarkand? It was
That time of Utopia by the text. Eagerly,
We crowded on the promise of a legend, found
A straw masquerade, the terminus of Party lies,
Inhuman patience that began in Moscow's streets
And wound through regulations and officialdom
To stagnate in Flecker's land of dreams.

There were no chants extolling market wares.
The bloom we sought in peasant cheeks
Was lodged in hoards of produce crushed against

Deep warehouse vaults – tubers, pears, deep purple
Aubergines, ponderous cabbages and lean spices.
Destination – Party ranks and dachas by the sea.
The shine we sought upon their skin was locked
In racked tomatoes, straight from still-life canvases,
In melon sphericals, like new-discovered worlds.
A wild assault of rare, exotic fruits flared
Our questing nostrils, mocked the mien of stiff
Official guides, breezes from a different time and place –
We did ask questions; received responses by the text.

Joy had fled the faces of the eternal women.
They lined the market outskirts, silently,
Winter twigs, dark shadows framed in rags
Limp greens outstretched, limp socks and shawls –
The regulation surplus they could hawk at will
For those few kopeks they would call their own.
A market! And no human sounds? We bade adieu
To Samarkand; we shared the train that hauled
Her missing cries to Moscow's hidden stores.

From frying-pan to furnace, from Slough of Despond
To turbid ponds named law of market forces
That makes the outlaw Bullfrog of the bog – I dread
A Mafia kingdom where Samarkand is but
Another tame protectorate, yet on parade
As a consumer's paradise, where one will yearn
For those bedraggled hands of dead Utopia.
Their merchandise was theirs – to make and sell
Their leisure moments knit the shawl and spun the lace
Carved the likeness or grotesque of dreams.
Each offering was a flight from drudgery, a cunning hour

Defiant of lies, of regulations that imposed conformity.
At worst, a pittance earned, an elixir of escape.

I spurn this double counterfeit – wages earned
In goods from plant assemblage – brassieres,
Jars of mayonnaise, jockstraps, plated cutlery, diapers,
Negligées and curtain rods, shaving cream, deodorants
Tourist wares, the ever-replicating *babushka* . . .
Where barter is debased, and leisure must be shared
In after hours converting wages-merchandise
To a common currency devalued from the source.
O Samarkand, your workers must prove traders too?
Accosting strangers, plying second-tier exchange
Lest the home be starved! Samarkand,
What bargain you have made! Utopia sold for this?
Will Chernobyl pay wageless scientists
In enriched uranium, to solve the state's insolvency?

Or maybe – as Allah wills – since soul and sale
Have ever shared their space – Samarkand
Will turn the other sort, twin face of that
Tarnished paradise whose sauce for goose
Was not for gander. We bid adieu to
Kulak, comprador, bourgeois deviationist
Revisionist capitalist running dog false consciousness
And allied Gulag overtures that masked
The silent guest in every home. That doomsday
Noise is stilled. New heroes of the revolution
Hail the anointed text, now simplified, that reads:
Holy or unclean. Taboos proliferate.
Like the bazaars of Beirut, Algiers
Or Teheran, will a store display, an order form,
'Satanic' music, poster, a fable on a tapestry,

A catalogue of books, second-hand merchandise
A dog-eared copy of *Arabian Nights*, a pamphlet poem –
Prove the trader's violent passport into paradise?

IV

The bazaars of the *souk* may prove denuded
The magic carpet folded out of sight, in dread.
There may be new commissars on patrol
Messengers between the laity and Deity.
The scrambled word that passes censorship is –
Kill. Kill the unveiled, for the word is veiled
To all but the anointed few, dacoits of Deity.

They sanctify the blade, still dripping from its last jihad
It carves a path through an old man's neck, but
The moving finger writes . . . though the ink of Kandahar
Has turned to blood. The heir of ancient dynasties
Of letters . . . Khorassan, Alexandria, Timbuktoo . . . lies
    sprawled
In the dirt and dust of a passageway.

He is no alien. No roots than his grow deeper
In that market place, no eye roved closer home.
He is that fixture in the market-place café
Sipping sweetened cups of mint, oblivious to
The bitter one that would be served
By the shadowy one, the waiter-stalker, a youth
Fed on dreams of sarabands of houris,
Doe-eyed virgins, wine and sweetmeats in the afterlife –
But to this paradise a key – the plunging knife.

    It's time to raise the rafters, time
    To chant the primal sanctity of man

Beyond coarse politics, beyond meagreness
Of race and faith, time to disinherit
Nationhood, episcopacies – we declare
This questing biped heir to cosmic legacies.
Who kills for love of god kills love, kills god,
Who kills in name of god leaves god
Without a name.

The market place of hate is quartered on the pious tongue
But this the old man knew, yet kept his daily tryst
With haggling cries, mock wars of merchandise
Mint tea and gossip, an avocation to observe and chronicle.
He shares the dreams of Samarkand
With traders and the traded, with sinners
And the sinned against,
With infidels and the self-assured of paradise –
A dream that never ends, a glimpse that still recedes,
That shimmering Golden Road to Samarkand.

v

The ocean meets the sea in a market place
And rivers ground their debris on its shelves –
Rich silt, beachcombers' treasure trove.
The rainbow's arc is rounded in a market place
Where scattered tribes of a busy world unite
Amidst the silenced blades of swords and spears
And ancient muskets, poison shafts and knobkerries.
Like guardians to that lost, miraculous edition,
Filled with lost wisdoms, lost journeys of the mind.
The space of dreams remain inviolate,
Egalitarian in the market place
Though desecration stalks in priestly garb
By surrogates, by one-eyed arbiters.

But now we share the strange and marvellous,
Indulge in thoughts of origin. We people artefacts
From ivory, skin and herbs, from aromatic wood,
Sifts of powder guaranteed for ailments old and new
Dark mysteries in clay jars, beauty gels,
Love potions, the lost gems of the world
And many more with fake lustre, fake patina –
Like fake piety, they exact veneration – still,
In the market place, their patina is peace, and
Though innocence be sometimes lost or counterfeited,
We share the gods of distant lands, of ancient times
And the Market Muse by whose decree
The knives are sheathed, and guns
Are mostly spiked, or fallen silent.

You who have heard the ocean waves,
Or the cries of dead mariners from bleached
Muteness of shell and conch, learn also
Other sounds beneath the market wares
And haggling voices – siren songs from coral beads,
A child's initiation wail in barks of camwood, a priest's
Liturgy in rosaries of sandalwood, a chieftain's
Ululation in horsetail whisks and beaded canes.

Dirges of bereavement seep through ancient mats,
The ochre-smeared antique, or a faded photograph –
The frame of tarnished silver will be home
Soon to a stranger's face, in an alien household.
And thus, we jostle strangers who turn guests and kin –
The market is that kind of meeting place.

The world is a market place – thus goes the song.
At close of market, in a sombre light,

Our feet will lead the way
Homewards, when eyes have closed for ever
On the next market day, and the indigo throng
Of all *orisa* wait to lead
Each seeker by the hand, into that last sanctuary
Across the arch of shadows.

One market day, in the *souk* of Cairo,
The zealot's counterfeiting hand did not triumph.
The moving finger writes, and having writ . . . the mind
Survives to sing the way on the Golden Road
Where dreams of Samarkand outlive
Tomorrow's market day.

Elegies

THE CHILDREN OF THIS LAND

The children of this land are old
Their eyes are fixed on maps in place of land
Their feet must learn to follow
Distant contours traced by alien minds
Their present sense has faded into past.

The children of this land are proud
But only seeming so. They tread on air but –
Note – the land it was that first withdrew
From touch of love their bare feet offered. Once,
It was the earth of their belonging.
Their pointed chins are aimed,
Proud seeming, at horizons filled with crows.
The clouds are swarms of locusts.

The children of this land grow the largest eyes
Within head sockets. Their heads are crowns
On neat fish spines, whose meat has passed
Through swing doors to the chill of conversation
And chilled wine. But the eyes stare dead
They pierce beyond the present through dim passages
Across the world of living.

These are the offspring of the dispossessed,
The hope and land deprived. Contempt replaces
Filial bonds. The children of this land
Are castaways in holed crafts, all tortoise skin
And scales – the callus of their afterbirth.
Their hands are clawed for rooting, their tongues
Propagate new social codes, and laws.

A new race will supersede the present –
Where love is banished stranger, lonely
Wanderer in forests prowled by lust,
On feral pads of power,
Where love is a hidden, ancient ruin, crushed
By memory, in this present
Robbed of presence

But the children of this land embrace the void
As lovers. The spores of their conjunction move
To people once human spaces, stepping nimbly
Over ghosts of parenthood. The children of this land
Are robed as judges, their gaze rejects
All measures of the past. A gleam
Invades their dead eyes briefly, lacerates the air
But with one sole demand:
Who sold our youth?

TOWER CLOCK: AKE REVISITED

Because the weary eyes hold no more light
Hands gouged them out, from all four faces
Of Ake's tower clock. The sockets' shame
Is sealed in slabs of bronze. These were once
Eyes of equity, hands that nudged
Sonorities from the belfry to embrace
All faiths, from hill to valley of Abeokuta
Keeping eternal vigil on the land of rocks.

Should it matter that the tower clock
No longer tells the time, its hands arrested
Like the hands of God in mid-creation?
Whose dare is this that seals
All faces of the compassed spire
In ponderous slabs of bronze?

It was, still is, the landmark of my youth.
I never can see kites but soar with them
Investing towers of every land, as they this spire
And with them hover, swoop and nest.
Who was this architect that thought
To blind the fourfold face of time?

Oh busy builder, have you never wished
Time would stand still, immovable
As Olumo Rock? Never slowed your pulse
Beneath the shade of such gaunt sanctuaries
Secure from tumbrils of a hasty world? Never
Drawn strength from stillness, serenity
From the voice of silence?

Overseer of birth registers, weddings,
Funerals and festive anthems, its cathedral womb
Pulsed to bellows of the asthmatic organ, arbitrated
Discords of choir at practice, and the Sunday homily.
Stolid watch over harvest offerings, anniversaries – it was
The Town Crier of New Year's Eve, bringing farm
To city, then, at daytime, posed its freckled whiteness
To offset chromatic swirls of each year's rebirth.

Yes, once, it tolled the hours, rang the half-hour
On cue, till the arm wearied, fell from hour
To half-hour in seconds, prey to gravity.
Then came the weary climb to zenith, timed –
As one in secret orbit with the sun –
To meet the hour's exactitude, foreshadowing
How we all shall keep tryst with infirmity
Fall, rise, fall and rise again, till the final weight
Of earth that brooks no shifting.

Requiescat in pace, tower, spire, bronze blinded
But thrust in the memorial sky, age-mottled yet ageless,
Still the landmark of our youth and, since memory
Is fickle – sleepless eye of vigils, mute notary,
Immemorial cenotaph.

LOW-COST HOUSING

Wrapped in flirtatious blades of grass,
You'll find them, derelict sentinels, where lizards
Conduct their blatant rapes, metronomic heads ablaze.
These are the planners' masterpieces –
Shelter for all by the new millennium –
Low-cost housing schemes, lowly and costly –
Long on invoices and short on shelter . . .

But yes, they house the rodents, reptiles, passive
Denizens of wood and undergrowth, dumb observers
Patient browsers. These beasts are not so dumb.
Their retreat was ever tactical, schooled to out-wait
Mendacities of appropriation. Rhetorical designs
Approved, contracted, ostentatious turning of the sod
To camera lights and drums and buntings, then,
Abortion at the drawing board. Drains outlined,
Roofs pencilled in, token beds of cement will become
Archaeological puzzles for future digs.

Your beasts are perennial squatters, reclaiming
Space that was ever theirs. The jungle lushly
Covers tracks from Abuja to the Central Bank.

ELEGY FOR A NATION

for Chinua Achebe, at seventy

I

Ah, Chinua, are you grapevine wired?
It sings: our nation is not dead, not clinically
Yet. Now this may come as a surprise to you,
It was to me. I thought the form I spied
Beneath the frosted glass of a fifty-carat catafalque
Was the face of our own dear land – 'own', 'dear',
Voluntary patriotese, you'll note – we try to please.
An anthem's sentiment upholds the myth.

Doctors IMF, World Bank and UNO refuse, it seems,
To issue a certificate of death – if debtors die
May creditors collect? We shall turn Parsees yet,
Lay this hulk in state upon the Tower of Silence,
Let vultures prove what we have seen, but fear to say –
For if Leviathan is dead, we are the maggots
Probing still her monstrous womb – one certainty
That mimics life after death. Is the world fooled?
Is this the price of hubris – to have dared
Sound Renaissance bugles for a continent?

Time was, our gazes roamed the land, godlike,
Pronounced it good, from Lagos to Lake Chad.
The ghosts of interlopers would be exorcised,
Not throwing the baby out with the bathwater, but –
Enthroning ours as ours, bearing names
Lodged in marrow of the dead, attesting lineage.
Consecrated brooms would sweep our earth
Clean of usurpers' footprints. We marched

To drums of ancient skins, homoeopathic
Beat against the boom of pale-knuckled guns.
We vied with the regal rectitude of Overamwen –
No stranger breath – he swore – *shall desecrate*
This hour of communion with our gods! We
Died with the women of Aba, they who held
A bridgehead against white levy, armed with pestle,
Sash and spindle, and a potent nudity – eloquent
Abomination in the timeless rites of wrongs.

Grim cycle of embattled years. Again we died
With miners of Iva valley who undermined
More than mere seams of anthracite. All too soon,
Alas, we would augment, in mimic claims,
In our own right, the register of martyrs. Oh,
How we've exercised the right of righteous folly
In defence of alien rhetoric ... *what God has joined*,
    etcetera.
For God, read white, read slaver surrogates.

We scaled the ranges of Obudu, prospected
Jos Plateau, pilgrims on rock-hills of Idanre.
Floated on pontoons from Bussa to silt beds
Of eternal Niger, reclaimed the mangrove swamps,
Startling mudskipper, manatee, and mermaids.
Did others claim the mantle of discoverers?
Let them lay patents on ancestral lands, lay claim
To paternity of night and day – ours
Were hands that always were, hands that pleat
The warp of sunbeam and the weft of dew,
Ours to create the seamless out of paradox.

In the mind's compost, meagre scrub yielded
Silos of grain. Walled cities to the north were
Sheaths of gold turbans, tuneful as minarets.
The dust of Durbars, pyrotechnic horsemen
And sparkling lances, all one with the ring of anvils
From Ogun's land to Ikenga's. Rainbow beads, *jigida*
From Bida's furnaces vied across the sky with
Iyun glow and Ife bronzes, luscent on ivory arches
Of Benin. Legend lured Queen Amina to Moremi,
Old scars of strife redeemed in tapestries
Of myth, recreating birthpang, and rebirth. And, yes –

We would steal secrets from the gods. Let Sango's axe
Spark thunderstones on rooftops, we would swing
In hawser hammocks on electric pylons, pulse through
    cities
In radiant energies, surge from battery racks to bathe
Town and hamlet in alchemical light. Orisa-oko
Would heal with herbs and scalpel. Ogun's drill
Was poised to plumb the earth anew, spraying aloft
Reams of rare alloys. Futurists, were we not
Annunciators of the Millennium long before its advent?
In our now autumn days, behold our leaden feet
Fast welded to the starting block.

Vain griots! Still, we sang the hennaed lips and fingers
Of our gazelle womenfolk, fecund Muses tuned
To Senghorian cadences. We grew filament eyes
As heads of millet, as flakes of cotton responsive
To brittle breezes, wraith-like in the haze of Harmattan.
Green of the cornfields of Oyo, ochre of groundnut
    pyramids
Of Kano, indigo in the ancient dye-pots of Abeokuta
Bronzed in earth's tonalities as children of one deity –

We were the cattle nomads, silent threads through
Forestries and cities, coastland and savannah,
Wafting Maiduguri to the sea, ocean mist to sand dunes.

Alas for lost idylls. Like Levi jeans on youth and age,
The dreams are faded, potholed at joints and even
Milder points of stress. Ghosts are sole inheritors.
Silos fake rotundity – these are kwashi-okor blights
Upon the landscape, depleted at source. Even
The harvest seeds were long devoured. Empty hands
Scrape the millennial soil at planting.

But Chinua, are you grapevine wired? Do you
Tune in, listen? There is old music in the air.
The word is out again, out from the closet.
Renaissance beats are thumbed in government lairs,
In lobbies, caucuses, on promotion posters,
In parliaments. Academe's close behind. Renaissance
Haunts beer and *suya* bar, street and rostrum,
Inhaled as tobacco smoke, chewed as kola,
Clerics beatify the word, lawyers invoke it.
Never word more protean, poised to incarnate
In theses, conferences, investments. A historic lure
Romances the Diaspora. Gang-raped, the continent
Turns pregnant with the word – it's sworn, we shall be
Born again, though we die in the attempt.

But then, *our* offsprings, Chinua, have they leisure
To play at love? To commune with Source, shaded
By coarse-grain village walls at noon? Crush wild mint
Between their fingers, let the *agbayun* coat
Their tongues, at war with the bitterness of kola?
Raid the hoards of gods and ancients,

Recite their lineage praise-names, clan histories?
Or have the rigours of survival bred a race
Of naked predators? Is sharing out of fashion?
Community a dirty word, service an obscenity?
Are ours the emerging children of Molucca
Born to burn at six, slaughter at seven,
Rinse their hand in the throat's death gurgle,
Secure in the arch-priest's absolution? Attuned
At noon to dissolution of the bond of dawn, deaf
To neighbour cries? Easy reddened are the wafers
Of communion – have we been here before?

Still, here you sit before the travelled world, gathered
To pay homage. Survived the kwashi-okor days.
You've fed on roots, barks and leaves
Your world contracted, ringed with iron
Fenced with the wringing hands of the world
As unctuous in neutrality as Pontius Pilate.
But you made flesh what is so often said –
Sweet are the uses of adversity – as even now
Your silent eloquence attests. The ancient pot-stills
Turned refineries. Neglected herbs, mystery silica
Powered transistors to accuse the world, screaming
We are not dead, but dying. And iron monsters
Rose furtively from forest bays, hammered
From the forges of Awka. Who can forget the errant
Ogbunikwe that rose skywards, plunged to blast
A fiery tunnel through encircling steel?

Absences surround your presence – he
The great town crier, Okigbo, and other griots
Silenced in infancy. The xylophones of justice

Chime much louder than the flutes of poets,
Their sirens lure the bravest to their doom.
But some survive, and survival breeds, it seems,
Unending debts. Time is our usurer, but earth remains
Sole signatory to life's covenant – and thus I ask:
Whose feet are these upon the storehouse loft?
Shod in studded boots or jewelled sandals,
Khaki crisp or silk embroidered – who are these?

Did time appoint these bailiffs? Behold
Enforcers out of time, shorn of memory but –
Crowned are the hollow skulls, signets on talons.
Their advent is the hour of locusts – behold
Cheeks in cornucopia from the silos' depletion
While the eyes of youth sink deeper in despair.
Death bestrides the streets, rage rides the sun
And hope is a sometime word that generations
Never learnt to spell.

Chinua, I think with you I dare
Be indelicate – we scrape our feet upon
The threshold of mortal proof, denying
The ancestors yet awhile our companionship –
May that day learn patience from afar! –
On the stage at Bard, behind the lectern,
Gazing across time to your staunch spirit
Wedded to a contraption we neither make nor mend
My irreverent thoughts were – There sits the nation,
All faculties intact, but wheelchair bound.
Your lesson of the will, alas, a creative valour
Marks the gulf between you and that land
We claim our own.

II

There are wonders in that land, Chinua
Are you wired? Tuned to images of cyber age?
Severed wrists will soon adorn our walls
And Conrad's *Heart of Darkness* be fulfilled.
The cairn of stones is building for the first
Butchery in a public square, a female scapegoat
Tethered for primordial rites that men devise
To keep their womenfolk obedient to the laws of man.

An encampment is on the move, biped
Amorphous tents, a sorcerer invasion choreographed
In castration shrouds, visors no less secretive
Than face-masks, twin to ancestral masquerades
Proclaimed infidel. They slink through streets
And markets – yes, it is our women on the move
Our mothers, wives and sisters, comrades-in-arms
Bereft of limbs and faces, *haute couture* decreed
By encyclicals of eunuch priests. Features
Mummified by laws of terror. Oh my compatriots,
Shaved bare-skull at initiation, convertites
Dipped body and soul in the waters of salvation
Are yours these zombies of the age, are these
The paracletes of the new millennium?

They'll murder heritage in its timeless crib,
Decree our heroes, heroines out of memory
Obliterate the narratives of clans, names
That bind to roots, reach to heavens, our
Links to ancestral presences. The Born-Agains
Are on rampage, born against all that spells
Life and mystery, legend and innovation.
Imprecations rend the air, song is taboo,

The stride of sun-toned limbs racing wind a sin,
Flesh is vile, wine, the gift of earth, execrated.
These tyrants have usurped the will of God.
How did we fail to learn, that guns and boots
Are not essential to a *coup d'état*?

Shall *Ala* die? *Ahiajoku* be anathematised? Does
Oya defile her streams, *Ifa* obstruct the paths
Of learning and councils of the wise? *Praise the Lord*
And launch the bulldozer – they've razed
The statues of *mbari* to the ground, these
Christian Talibans. Their brothers in Offa
Murder *Moremi* in her shrine, shrieking *Allah akbar*.
Rivals else, behold their bonded zeal that sanctifies
Alien rape of our quiescent Muses, extolling theirs.

We who neither curse their gods nor desecrate
Their texts, their prayer mats or altars –
What shall we do, Chinua, with these hate clerics?
While we sleep, their fingers spread as brambles,
Deface our Book of Life. How teach them:

Some are born pagan, wedded to life's seamlessness
Tuned to the breath of things, magma and animus.
The waters of the Holy Gospel bounced against
This splinter of Olumo Rock, retreated
In despair, seeking more porous earth. How reveal
The sublimity of godhead that abhors
The murdering tyranny of Creed? Has gore
Proved godlove on Kaduna streets – ten thousand
Mutilations and three thousand dead of faith?
But the sun rose still the following dawn, indifferent.

Let all creeds be recast. If the gates of Paradise
Are locked behind the Pope's demise,
We wish him blessed occupancy of yonder realms
With all the Heavenly Host. Has the last Imam
Been here and gone? Then, *Bon Voyage*
Seek me out among the questers, creed-divorced,
In covenant only to that solvent that is earth.

How shall they be taught, Chinua, that Ajapa
Lives, but no longer borrows feathers from the birds
To survey earth? Myths are our wise cohabitants. Icarus
Transcended wax, new trajectories lace the spheres.
The galaxy is boundless host to a new race
Of voyagers, seeking the once forbidden. Cinders
From Promethean dares, shards of Ajapa's shell,
Are constellations by which ships of space are steered.

The jealous gods are no more. Age by age
We inched towards the sun, then raced beyond
To drink the heady draught of space, returned to earth
Emboldened. The voices of new prophets are not voided
In the wilderness but fulfilled. Applause
Is the new music of the spheres – it's heard
In other lands, I am told. I have not heard it here.

But we survived, Chinua. And though survival reads
Unending debt – for time, alas decrees us
Witnesses, thus debtors – earth alone remains
Our creditor. Yet I fear the communion pots
Lie broken at the crossroads, kola nuts and cowries
Scattered by scavengers. Couriers turn coat,
Turned by profit, priest, predator and politician.

The masquerade's falsetto may reveal, not
Artifice but loss of voice, its gutturals camouflage

Death throes, not echoes of our spirit realms.
The strongest eagle, wing-span clipped, talons
Manicured in gilded thumbscrews may not hold
Nor bear the weight of sacrifice. Our caryatids
Are weary of cycles of endless debts. Incense
Of burnt offering, heavy with abominations
Hangs close to altar, dissipates between Earth
And Sky. Shorn of new alibis, our intercessors
Falter at the door of judgement. What shall we say
To the years that drift past, accusing?
What shall we chant to their dew-bright notes –
Our new tuned buglers of the Renaissance?

VAIN RANSOM

for the dead and maimed of Kenya and Tanzania

The price their forebears paid, it seems
Has not sufficed as ransom for this
Future – stillborn, a past in perpetual labour –
Not though their bones have whitened
Dunes of sand, paved caravan routes
Since memory began. Not though their prayers
Were swallowed bosoms deep within
The Atlantic, their marrow sucked to feed
Sea monsters, the manhood of a continent
Lost to white knives in a Brave New World.

Salt of the earth, for so they must be deemed who,
Wedded to iron, embraced the salty waves
Chanting, *Deliverance, Deliverance!* Who
Mined the salt of the Tigris marshlands;
And spice of life, lashed to argosies of cloves,
And dates and cinnamon from Dar es Salaam
Across the Indian Ocean. And were theirs not the sinews
Of sweetness in cane plantations, from isle to isle
To land mass of the Americas? And cotton fingers
Fettered to imperious looms of the world?

Then, for a new deliverance, sutured the Kenyan
Forests with legend, elusive wraiths of night and day
Who bathed the land in their valiant potion, raised
The tumultuous concert whose enduring chorus –
Uhuru! – rose as anthem of a continent.

Still, this does not suffice. The rage of blood resumes
And quarrels old and new of distant lands are settled

On our earth at somnolence. Blind and blinding rivalries
Come to a grim, sneak reckoning on scars
Yet vibrant on deep-earthed skulls of memory.

Or maybe – since this penance past does not suffice –
We must seek answers in recurrent pacts
Of self-immolation – Liberia, Congo, Somalia,
Sierra Leone, Rwanda and all – that these
Entice as flies to carrion, urge alien hands to augment
Our amplitude of death? That the incontinent roll-call
Of ruler-predators, contemptuous of their kind
Has called to kindred jackals from afar to a feast
Of deathliness, the corpse of hope laid out
On a continent's permissive board?

We, the children of disdain, infidels of earth,
When we seek – like they – our turn
Upon the throne of justice, let that mantra
Be now silenced that has reigned till now –
The end shall justify the means – and allied canticles.
Let our shrines and wished-for palaces
Be not founded yet again upon the peace
Of innocence. Let not evil call to evil in a ring
Of Time's entrapment, a wheel of fire and blood
Whose spinning will consume at will

Forgive me – deafened by the flap of kindred souls
That fled these skies, tuned to the timeless tumulus
Of Kilimanjaro, Idanre, I lost the answer to that question
That the Unborn, and my Ancestors bade me ask:
What god do you presume to serve?

For I know not yours, nor will revere it, nor hail
The blasphemy of wars named holy, yet do I

Bid you welcome at my hearth and shrine. Immaculate
Your ablutions, though reeking with the blood
Of our one universe of kith, kin, and stranger,
The not-so-immaculate in your sacred reckoning.

Enough of this disdain! Shed your masquerade,
The nuptial weeds of fear. Sheathe your hand
That lashes out in contempt of humankind. Take mine,
Unwashed, while it still celebrates
The sacred mass of life.

At the Garden of Remembrance, Nairobi, 8 February 2001